T1D

Cooking Ahead For Kids With Type 1 Diabetes

Arianna Guinn

El Monito Enterprises

Disclaimer

I am not a doctor. This publication is for informational purposes only, based on my own research and experience. It has not been evaluated by the FDA or the medical profession. It was not written to replace any advice from your medical practitioner. I and the publisher, assume no responsibility or liability whatsoever on the behalf of any purchaser or reader of these materials. Please consult your primary care physician before beginning any program of nutrition, exercise, or remedy.

Introduction

The purpose of this book is to try to make it easier for children and adults to stick to a diet recommended by their doctors and dieticians. I've put together some ideas, recipes, and plans that I hope will make living with diabetes a much less daunting task until a cure can be found.

Table of Contents

All About Justin

On April 16, 2008, my grandson Justin was diagnosed with Type 1 Diabetes. He had been complaining of a bellyache, and was not being his usual, active self. We chalked it up to, "Probably just a bug." He had no other symptoms that seemed extraordinary, but he didn't get better. Blood tests were done and we were given the bad news. It all happened very quickly.

I knew there was a difference between Types 1 and 2 Diabetes, but never really paid much attention because I was familiar with Type 2. From my experience with Type 2, I knew it could generally be controlled with diet and exercise.

Then I learned what Type 1 really was and I was horrified. Justin's mother (my daughter) and I discussed his disease and convinced ourselves that it could have been much worse. It is a life changing but controllable disease, and we felt fortunate that it hadn't been a more serious disease like cancer. No child should have to face any deadly disease, but millions do, and many do not survive. We made up our minds that this would only be a hiccup in his life. His mother has been totally devoted to him. With two other children and a full-time job, sometimes I think it's harder on her than it is on him.

He's thirteen now, and from my experience (years of driving a school bus), thirteen-year-olds just seem to have no sense. Trying to keep sugar levels stable and steady is a frustrating task and an even bigger challenge when you throw puberty into the mix. He has a lot going for him, being active, athletic, and in general good health, which is something to be grateful for.

Cooking Ahead – The Plan

The purpose of this chapter is to simplify portions and counting, along with teaching young people how to measure and portion out snacks ahead of time so things are ready when you want or need them. Not just snacks, but meals too. If menus and meals are prepared in advance, it's easy to microwave something and less likely to grab something that is bad for you because there may not be enough time to prepare a proper meal.

Going along with the same ideas in my previous book, Cooking Ahead – The Less Stress Way To Cook For 2 To 200, make a list of foods that are good choices, what they like to eat, and acceptable carb counts. Try to stick to a heart-healthy diet also, so going into adulthood, they don't end up with cardiovascular disease; that would be a real kick in the you-know-what!

Buy snack-sized bags and portion out a week's worth of snacks. Some should be for on-the-go, some frozen or refrigerated for home, and some marked, "FOR EMERGENCY USE ONLY!" for those low sugar issues that sometimes happen. If there are other family members, don't forget snacks or meals for them or they may dip into the "special" stuff. My daughter keeps Justin's snacks and meals in a separate container.

Plan for a week's worth of meals and cook enough for the work/school week. A diabetic diet is actually a pretty healthy diet so maybe the rest of the family might benefit too, plus the child would probably feel better with company on his diet, not being resentful of everyone else eating french fries!

This may seem like a hassle, but I've been cooking ahead for years and two to three hours on a Sunday equates to much more time saved throughout the week and much less stress.

I researched and shopped for groceries, picking up items I thought kids would enjoy, reading nutritional values and incorporating some special "no-no" treats into snack ideas so they wouldn't feel deprived. Justin saw the bag of chocolate miniatures and lit up. With only 5 carbs in one little bar, it's a tasty treat!

We then had a Justin Day. I got out my collection of foods and we sampled. A few things weren't cared for, but a lot was surprising. He's been to camp and knows how to portion (an extremely important word). I think kids should be encouraged to help cook and prepare their meals and snacks. It gives them ownership and a sense of accomplishment. Sorry, that was the bossy mom in me.

The whole family was there for dinner and we had spaghetti and meatballs and seafood linguini (recipes to follow). I didn't tell them until later that it was all low-carb diet food.

I know some people are not much into cooking or just don't have the time so I tried to keep it simple. Kids have different tastes so I tried to encompass a variety of things, not just what Justin liked. Another tip is to garnish. It's been said that the psychological effect of foods that look good generally taste better.

Adults with T1D who still continue to struggle with their diet, like my friend Jim, will find this plan helpful. He is living proof (around fifty years old) that it is a very survivable disease. He was diagnosed when he was twenty nine years old. It was tough because he was so used to a normal life for so long.

I kept the nutritional values simple, only focusing on the big four. Calories. Fat. Protein. Carbs.

Essential and helpful kitchen tools.
Scale – this is essential for proper portion control. It doesn't need to be expensive.
Measuring cups – liquid and dry weight.
Measuring spoons.
Snack bags.
Various airtight containers.
A good blender.
Quality thermos for food, not drinks.

Breakfast

They say it's the most important meal of the day. Make sure you keep to your designated amount of carbs and follow your nutritionist's or dietician's guidelines. Here are some recipes that we found tasty. It's much easier to follow a diet if it tastes good.

EGGS

They have been called the perfect food. They have been loved and hated. I think they have a place in a healthy diet. I like them and they are easy to prepare.

Fried, scrambled (add a teaspoon of milk and whisk with a fork), over-medium, or over-hard using vegetable spray on low/medium heat.

Soft boiled – cover egg with water in cooking pan and bring to a boil. Start counting as soon as the water begins to boil. Three minutes later, done! I remember putting the eggs in little cups shaped like chickens and cutting the tops off, dipping my toast into the yolks.

Calories – 70. Fat – 5. Protein – 6. Carbs – 0

Frittatas

Serving – 1 muffin

A Frittata is a flat Italian style omelette that is usually prepared in a cast iron skillet. My preference for making these ahead is muffin style. I have also poured the mixture into a baking dish and cut it into bread-sized squares and made sandwiches.

12 large eggs
12 ounces lean ham
6 ounces shredded cheese

Whisk eggs in large bowl, just enough to mix well. Do not over whisk or they will overflow in the muffin tins. Chop ham into fine pieces, add ham and cheese to eggs. Spray standard 12 cup Teflon coated muffin tin with cooking spray. Fill each cup (pretty much to the top of each cup). Bake in preheated oven for 20 minutes at 350°.

You may add any type of spice or hot sauce as you mix it up. I like it spicy so I added 1 tablespoon of chopped chipotle peppers in adobe sauce.

Any type of meat or veggies may be used, ham just has a good consistency, and I like ham. Just remember to adjust the nutritional values with different ingredients.

Calories – 165. Fat – 9.5. Protein – 16. Carbs – 0.

Omelettes

1 large egg
2 ounce chopped ham
½ ounce cheese
1 teaspoon milk
salt and pepper to taste

Whisk egg with the salt and pepper and milk in a bowl. Pour into omelette pan (skillet with curved bottom edges) that has been sprayed with cooking spray on low/medium heat. When the egg sets, flip it over and add the ham and cheese and fold in half to form a pocket. Heat briefly. If serving immediately, let the cheese melt. If cooking ahead, remove the omelette as soon as you fold it over, let it cool on plate and place in container.

Adjust ingredients according to taste, but remember to adjust the portions and nutritional values accordingly!

Calories – 180. Fat – 15. Protein – 21. Carbs – 0

Scrambles

1 large egg
2 ounce chopped ham
½ ounce cheese
1 teaspoon milk
salt and pepper to taste

Whisk egg with salt and pepper and milk in a bowl. Stir in ham. Pour into sprayed skillet on low/medium heat. Stir until eggs set. Remove from skillet and top with cheese. If cooking ahead, add cheese when reheating.

Calories – 180. Fat – 15. Protein – 21. Carbs – 0.

Sammies and Burritos

These are great for making ahead, but keep the bread and contents separate. Assemble them after heating.

Breakfast Sammie Suggestions

Sandwich Thin with egg, bacon (2 slices, about 2 ounces), and cheese (1 ounce).

Calories – 370. Fat – 11. Protein – 10. Carbs – 18.

There are so many combinations, check out the bread suggestions in Chapter 7 – Sides & Breads, and pick one, then check out the Sammie Fixin's in Chapter 4 – Lunch & Dinner, and pick one of those. You'll have to get the calculator out and do some math. Sorry, but it's like going to Subway. If you're just looking at carbs, you generally just need to look at the bread but if you start putting crazy stuff on your sammie, like hash browns or potato chips, that's just more math!

Cereals and Fruit

Very high carbs, so watch the underlined portions. Most of the previous recipes have little or no carbs, so if you have an omelette, you could add some cereal and still not go over your carb limit. Justin was given a total of 30-45. There are way too many cereals and fruits to list, so check the packaging.

Meat and Eggs

This is like Sammie combinations, choose, prepare, and enjoy. I do this for my breakfast for the whole week, sometimes just meat, eggs, and cheese if I'm low carbing or making a sandwich. It takes me about twenty minutes for the week.

Don't forget to add onions, mushrooms, peppers, tomato, avocado, and spices if you like them. These are zero to low carb additions that add flavor.

Breakfast to most people means eggs and bacon. I myself am not a typical breakfast person. I prefer leftovers or whatever strikes my fancy. Just remember portions and nutritional facts.

Beverages

Get hooked on water. The more you drink, the more you'll love it.

Coffee – not really a kid's drink, but if a T1D does drink it, don't forget to count everything you put in it!

Tea – count the sugar.

Sugar – 1 teaspoon
Calories – 15. Fat – 0. Protein – 0. Carbs – 4.

Stevia
Calories – 0. Fat – 0. Protein – 0. Carbs – 0.

Milk – 8 ounces
Calories – 150. Fat – 8. Protein – 8. Carbs – 12.

Orange Juice – 8 ounces
Calories – 100. Fat – 0. Protein – 1. Carbs – 24.

V8 – 11.5 ounces
Calories – 70. Fat – 0. Protein – 3. Carbs – 14.

V8 Strawberry-Banana Fusion – 8 ounces
Calories – 110. Fat – 0. Protein – 0. Carbs – 28.

Pineapple Juice – 8 ounces
Calories – 130. Fat – 0. Protein – 0. Carbs – 33.

Apple Juice – 8 ounces
Calories – 117. Fat – 0. Protein – 0. Carbs – 29.

Grapefruit Juice – 8 ounces
Calories – 115. Fat – 0. Protein – 1. Carbs – 28.

Grape Juice – 8 ounces
Calories – 154. Fat – 0. Protein – 1. Carbs – 38.

Hot Chocolate – 1 cup w/2% milk
Calories – 210. Fat – 6. Protein – 10. Carbs – 32.

Lunch and Dinner

These meals are interchangeable. Lunch has generally been "the cup of soup and a sandwich" meal. The lighter meal of the day. Dinner has been the bigger meal of the two. Medical professional opinions vary on this, but T1D's are generally directed to have more carbs at lunch.

The recipes that follow are generally low to zero carbs. Add bread and sides accordingly to achieve proper carb amounts set by your nutritionist.

Sammie Fixins

Kahn's Bacon – 1 slice (check label of your brand)
Calories – 60. Fat – 10. Protein – 6. Carbs – 0.

Lean Ham – 2 ounces
Calories – 60. Fat – 1. Protein – 10. Carbs – 0.

Roast Beef (lean) – 3 ounces
Calories – 195. Fat – 11. Protein – 23. Carbs – 0.

Lean Ground Beef, broiled or grilled – 3 ounces
Calories – 218. Fat – 14. Protein – 22. Carbs – 0.

Sausage – 4" X ¼" patty
Calories – 100. Fat – 8. Protein – 5. Carbs – trace

Deli Roast Beef (high quality) – 2 ounces
Calories – 80. Fat – 2.5. Protein – 15. Carbs – 0.

Deli Bologna – 2 ounces
Calories – 150. Fat – 13. Protein – 7. Carbs – 1.

Deli Salami – 2 ounces
Calories – 130. Fat – 11. Protein – 8. Carbs – 0.

Deli Chicken – 2 ounces
Calories – 60. Fat – 1. Protein – 13. Carbs – 0.

Kahn's Hot Dog – 1
Calories – 150. Fat – 13. Protein – 6. Carbs – 2.

Johnsonville Original Bratwurst – 1
Calories – 260. Fat – 21. Protein – 14. Carbs – 2.

Deli Style Cheeses – 1 ounce
Calories – 100. Fat – 8. Protein – 7. Carbs – 0.

Packaged Cheese – 1 slice
Calories – 70. Fat – 5. Protein – 4. Carbs – 2.

Basic Burgers

Serving size – 1 patty

Form 1 pound of lean ground beef into 3 patties of equal size. Using a scale and a burger press is very handy for this. You can also buy ready-made patties. Making them yourself is not only cheaper, but you can make variations on the basic burger.

Calories – 363. Fat – 23. Protein – 36. Carbs – 0.

Adding salt and pepper and sprinkling with Liquid Smoke won't change the nutritional values.

Variations

Thoroughly mix beef with the following, divide into 3 equal patties, and grill until fully cooked.

1 tablespoon finely chopped chipotle peppers in adobe sauce.

3 tablespoons taco seasoning.

¼ cup chopped mushrooms and/or ¼ cup chopped onions.

1/8 cup pizza sauce and 1/8 cup parmesan cheese.

1/8 cup habanero pineapple sauce.

1/8 cup German mustard.

These result in no or trace changes in nutritional values.

Burger or Sammie Toppers

Grilled Pineapple Slice
Calories – 38. Fat – 0. Protein – trace. Carbs – 10.

Onion Slice – 1/8" thick
Calories – 5. Fat – 0. Protein – trace. Carbs - <1.

Dill Pickles – Free
Calories – 0. Fat – 0. Protein – 0. Carbs – 0.

Tomato Slice – ¼ ' thick
Calories – 4. Fat – 0. Protein – trace. Carbs - <1.

Mustard – Free
Calories – 0. Fat – 0. Protein – 0. Carbs – 0.

Ketchup – 1 tablespoon
Calories – 20. Fat – 0. Protein – 0. Carbs – 5.

Hellman's Mayo – 1 tablespoon
Calories – 60. Fat – 6. Protein – 0. Carbs - <1.

A1 – 1 tablespoon
Calories – 15. Fat – 0. Protein – 0. Carbs – 3.

Baked Steak Burgers

Serving – 1 patty

Basic Burger recipe.
Standard gravy or sauce packet.

Prepare basic burger into three equal patties. Prepare sauce or gravy (like brown gravy or mushroom sauce) as directed on packet. Coat each burger with sauce and place in baking dish, pouring remaining sauce over burgers. Cover with foil and bake in preheated 350° oven for 1 hour.

This may then be eaten as-is, on a bun, open-faced sandwich, over low carb pasta, or over cooked cauliflower.

Calories – 378. Fat – 23. Protein – 36. Carbs – 3.

Recalculate values when combining with something else. Example: add values for buns if eating as sandwiches.

Beanless Chili

4 – 1 cup servings

1 pound beef
1 can chili style tomatoes
½ small chopped onion
Optional: crumbled Cheez-Its, Goldfish Crackers, or tortilla chips.
½ ounce shredded cheese.
Don't forget to add these values.

Brown ground beef in sauce pan. Drain. Add onions to the meat and sauté until translucent (about 2 minutes). Add tomatoes and simmer about 45 minutes to 1 hour. Add optional items and cheese.

May also be used for chili dogs.

Calories – 294. Fat – 17. Protein – 55. Carbs – 4.5.

Beef Stew

8 – 1 cup servings

Approx – 3 pounds lean beef (sirloin tip)
1 medium onion – chopped
1 small potato peeled and cubed
1 ½ cups cubed baby carrots
2 beef bouillon cubes
2 tablespoons olive oil
2 packets mushroom sauce or brown gravy

Cut beef into 1" cubes and brown in olive oil on medium heat in large saucepan. Add enough water to cover beef, bring to boil and reduce heat to low. Cover and cook until tender (about 1 ½ hours). Be careful not to cook dry. Add onions, carrots, and potatoes. Add water to cover if necessary. Cover, bring to a boil (add bouillon cubes), reduce to simmer and cook until carrots are tender (about 30 minutes). Drain and remove from pan. Make sauce in pan according to packets. When sauce is ready, return beef and veggies to pan, mix, and heat.

Calories – 312. Fat – 7. Protein – 40. Carbs – 9.

Grilled Steak

Cut a quality steak (at least Choice, Select is iffy) into 3 ounce servings, trimming the fat. Grill over medium/high heat (can be cooked under the broiler) until desired doneness is achieved.

For ½" thickness:
Medium Rare – 3/2 minutes
Medium – 2/3 minutes
Well – 5/3 minutes

For ¾" thickness:
Medium Rare – 4/3 minutes
Medium – 5/3 minutes
Well – 7/5 minutes

For 1" thickness:
Medium Rare – 5/4 minutes
Medium – 6/4 minutes
Well – 8/6 minutes

Let it rest 5 minutes before cutting.

Topping suggestions – Just plain steak goodness!

Seasoning salt and pepper and/or sprinkle with Liquid Smoke.

Cajun Rub

2 teaspoons salt
2 teaspoons garlic powder
2 ½ teaspoons smoke paprika
1 teaspoon black pepper
1 teaspoon onion powder
1 teaspoon cayenne
½ teaspoon oregano
½ teaspoon red pepper flakes (optional)

A1

With mortar and pestle, crush 1 teaspoon instant coffee to powder, mix with 2 teaspoons garlic salt and 1 teaspoon pepper. Sprinkle on steak.

Cut steak into bite-size pieces and mix with a side from Chapter 7, or serve whole with a salad.

Calories – 166. Fat – 6. Protein – 26. Carbs – 0.

Ground Beef Goulash

6 – 1 cup servings

2 pounds ground beef
14 ounce can diced tomatoes – zesty chili style
14 ounce can French style green beans (drained)

Brown ground beef in large saucepan, drain off all liquid. Stir in tomatoes and simmer for about 30 minutes. Add green beans and heat through.

Calories – 380. Fat – 16. Protein – 39. Carbs – 9.

Version Two

2 pounds ground beef
14 ounce can tomatoes – Italian style
1 ½ cups diced baby carrots
½ cup Parmesan cheese

Brown ground beef in large saucepan, drain off all liquid. Stir in tomatoes and carrots and simmer for about 30 minutes. Add Parmesan cheese and mix well.

Calories – 398. Fat – 20. Protein – 42. Carbs – 11.

Ground Beef w/Cauliflower Alfredo sauce

6 – 1 cup servings

2 pounds ground beef
1 medium head cauliflower
8 ounces lite sour cream
½ cup Parmesan cheese

Clean cauliflower and cut into pieces. Cover with water in medium saucepan and bring to boil. Reduce heat to low and cook until soft. Drain completely.

While cauliflower is cooking, brown ground beef in large skillet, allowing it to cook additional 2 minutes after browned. Drain all remaining liquid. With fork, mash cauliflower into ground beef.

In small bowl, mix sour cream and Parmesan cheese together. Mix everything well and simmer 10 minutes.

Eat as-is or with a small salad.

Calories – 560. Fat – 36. Protein – 58. Carbs – 7.

Meatballs

About 45 meatballs

1 pound ground beef
½ pound pork sausage
½ tablespoon basil
½ tablespoon oregano
¼ teaspoon garlic salt
¼ teaspoon onion powder
1 egg
½ bread heel – crumbled

Thoroughly mix all ingredients with your hands. Form into 1" balls. Slowly brown in 2 tablespoons olive oil.

Per meatball:

Calories – 40. Fat – 3. Protein – 5. Carbs – ¼.

Meatloaf

10 – 4 ounce servings

2 pounds ground beef
1 pound pork sausage
1 small onion – chopped
1 clove garlic – minced
2 eggs
1 bread heel – crumbled
2 tablespoon olive oil
8 ounces tomato sauce
Parmesan cheese

Sauté onions and garlic in olive oil about 5 minutes on low/medium heat. In large bowl, combine remaining ingredients except tomato sauce, mix thoroughly, and form into loaf. Place in greased 9" X 12" baking dish. Pour tomato sauce over, cover, and bake at 350° for 1 hour. Remove cover and bake for an additional 30 minutes. Remove from pan and let rest for 15 minutes before slicing.

Calories – 354. Fat – 24. Protein – 30. Carbs – 4.

Mongolian Beef

6 – 1 cup servings

1 ½ - 2 pounds sirloin steak
2 cups coarsely chopped broccoli
½ cup finely chopped onion
2 tablespoon olive oil
2 eggs
¼ cup Mongolian Sauce

Grill steak Medium Rare, let cool and slice in 1/8"
strips, 2" long. In a wok on medium heat, sauté
broccoli and onion, stirring often for about 5 minutes.
Add beef and heat through. Break eggs over mixture,
let set for a minute until eggs are cooked. Add
Mongolian Sauce.

Calories – 309. Fat – 12. Protein – 49. Carbs – 6.

Mongolian Sauce

6 – ¼ cup servings

1 teaspoon olive oil
½ teaspoon ginger powder
1 tablespoon minced garlic

½ cup soy sauce
½ cup water
1/8 cup brown sugar
½ teaspoon corn starch
cayenne pepper to taste

Warm oil in saucepan over medium/low heat. Add ginger and garlic, stirring quickly to avoid scorching. Add water, soy, corn starch, and brown sugar, allowing sugar to dissolve. Simmer to desired consistency. Add cayenne pepper.

Calories – 22. Fat – 0. Protein - >1. Carbs – 4.

A lot of people do not like onions, but it adds so much flavor. Chopped fine, they almost "disappear".

Pot Roast

8 servings

3 pounds beef roast (sirloin tip)
1 pound baby carrots
1 medium onion – coarsely chopped
10 ounce can onion soup
¼ cup red wine

Spray roasting pan with vegetable spray and place roast in pan. Bake at 350° for 2 – 3 hours until fork tender. Remove from pan to drain broth. Freeze broth in containers for future recipes requiring beef broth. Return roast to pan and add remaining ingredients with onion soup being poured over everything last. Cover and bake 1 more hour.

Per serving (approx 4 ounces beef)

Calories – 350. Fat – 7. Protein – 41. Carbs – 8.

Roast Beef

About 8 – 3 ounce servings

2 pounds beef roast (sirloin tip)
salt and pepper to taste

Bake in a baking bag in shallow pan at 350° for about 2 hours. Remove and let sit for 5 minutes before slicing, or put in fridge and slice when cold.

Calories – 195. Fat – 11. Protein – 23. Carbs – 0.

Seasoned Ground Beef for Tacos, Burritos, and Salad

6 – 3 ounce servings

1 pound lean ground beef
3 tablespoons Taco Seasoning
1 cup water

Brown and drain ground beef in medium skillet on medium heat. Add Taco Seasoning and water and mix thoroughly. Bring to boil, reduce heat and simmer for 20 minutes.

Calories – 229. Fat – 14. Protein – 22. Carbs – 3.

Taco Seasoning

3 tablespoons to 1 cup water = 6 servings

9 tablespoons corn starch
3 tablespoons chili powder
1 ½ teaspoon salt
1 ½ teaspoon pepper
¾ teaspoon garlic powder
¾ teaspoon onion powder

¾ teaspoon oregano
1 ½ teaspoon smoke paprika
1 ½ teaspoon cumin
1 ½ teaspoon cayenne pepper

Mix all together and store in airtight container.

Calories – 54. Fat – 0. Protein – 0. Carbs – 13.

Shredded Beef

12 – ½ cup servings

2 tablespoons olive oil
3 pounds sirloin tip or brisket
1 ½ teaspoon seasoning salt
1 ½ teaspoon pepper
2 tablespoons Liquid Smoke
1 large onion – chopped fine
¼ cup red wine
2 cups water

Rub all sides of meat with seasoning salt, pepper, and Liquid Smoke. Using a large skillet or Dutch Oven, brown meat on each side in olive oil on medium heat. Pour water over meat, cover and simmer 2 – 3 hours (add water as necessary so as not to cook dry). Remove from pan and let sit until easy to handle (I cut it into 4 or 5 big pieces to cool faster). Cook off any excess water in skillet and set skillet aside.

In pan drippings, sauté onions for about 4 minutes. Shred beef (while still warm) into pan, add wine, stir and simmer for about 30 minutes. Add water as necessary to keep from getting dry. Meat should be moist but not soupy.

Calories – 187. Fat – 4. Protein – 26. Carbs – 1.

Vegetable Soup

7 to 8 – 1 cup servings

3 pounds beef (sirloin tip)
15 ounce can diced tomato
1 ½ cup cubed fresh baby carrots
2 cups water
1 cup chopped fresh leeks (white with some green,
thoroughly wash – see note below)
1 cup celery heart with leaves
5 bouillon cubes
½ medium or small potato – cubed (see further note
below)
salt and pepper to taste

Cut beef into 1" cubes. Using large saucepan, brown meat in olive oil. Add water and bouillon cubes, bring to boil and simmer for about 1 ½ hours. Add leeks, celery, and tomato and cook another 45 minutes. Add carrots and potato and cook 30 minutes longer.

I like the long cook time for flavors to mix and liquid cooks down so soup is thicker.

Calories – 356. Fat – 8. Protein – 47. Carb – 8.

If you are not familiar with leeks, they are grown in sandy soil and should be sliced and washed thoroughly in a pan of water to get all soil out.

If you are cooking ahead for lunch (since more carbs are allowed at lunchtime), triple up on potatoes.

Chicken

Any time you are boiling or baking chicken, always save the broth and freeze in 8 or 16 ounce containers for use in other recipes. Make tastier dishes than some you would make using water instead.

Chicken Stew

6 – 1 cup serving depending on bird size

whole chicken
1 packet chicken gravy
1 ½ cups diced fresh baby carrots
½ medium potato or 1 small potato – cubed
1 medium onion – chopped fine
salt and pepper to taste

Spray covered casserole dish or roasting pan with vegetable spray. Place thoroughly washed whole bird in, and sprinkle with seasoning salt or salt and pepper. Bake at 350° for 1 ½ - 2 hours (chicken will be pulling away from bone when done). Remove and place on platter to cool. Cut open to cool faster. Remove meat from bone and tear into chunks.

Place veggies in large saucepan and cover with broth from chicken. Cook until fork tender. Drain broth. Add meat to veggies. Add packet to 1 cup chicken broth and stir into stew. Heat on low/medium heat until thickened.

Calories – 390. Fat – 17. Protein – 45. Carbs – 11.

Grilled Chicken

Serving size – 4 ounces of meat

chicken of your choice
salt or pepper to taste

If grilling chicken on the bone, you may want to bake in 350° oven for about 30 minutes first.

Make sure chicken is thoroughly cooked.

Boneless skinless breast:
Calories – 110. Fat – 1 ½. Protein – 23. Carbs – 0.

Boneless skinless thigh:
Calories – 170. Fat – 11. Protein – 17. Carbs – 0.

When your chicken is almost done, brush lightly with your favorite BBQ sauce. Count amount used toward total carb count.

Chipotle Chicken

1 serving – 4 ounces

4 boneless skinless chicken breast
4 tablespoons finely chopped chipotle peppers in
adobe sauce
4 ounces margarita mix
1 ounce tequila
8 slices smoked gouda – 1 ounce

Slice chicken breast in half lengthwise. Place chicken and remaining ingredients in a 1 gallon Ziploc bag and marinate in the fridge for at least 4 hours or overnight. Make sure to work the mixture into the chicken. Drain off all the liquid.

Grill on medium heat until thoroughly cooked, but be careful not to dry it out. 3 minutes per side should do. Top with cheese.

Calories – 235. Fat – 10 ½. Protein – 30. Carbs – 6.

Mongolian Chicken

6 – 1 cup servings

4 boneless skinless chicken breasts – cut into ½"
cubes
2 cups coarsely chopped broccoli
½ cup finely chopped onion
2 tablespoons olive oil
2 eggs
¼ cup Mongolian Sauce

In wok on medium heat with olive oil, cook chicken thoroughly (about 10 minutes, stirring every minute or so). Remove from pan and cook broccoli and onion for about 5 – 6 minutes in juices in pan, adding a little more oil if needed. Return chicken and heat through. Break eggs over mixture, let set for a minute until eggs are cooked. Add Mongolian Sauce.

Mongolian Sauce

6 – ¼ cup servings

1 teaspoon olive oil
½ teaspoon ginger powder
1 tablespoon minced garlic

½ cup soy sauce
½ cup water
1/8 cup brown sugar
½ teaspoon corn starch
cayenne pepper to taste

Warm oil in saucepan over medium/low heat. Add ginger and garlic, stirring quickly so as not to scorch. Add water, corn starch, soy, and sugar, allowing sugar to dissolve. Simmer until desired consistency is achieved. Add cayenne to taste.

Calories – 150. Fat – 3. Protein – 19. Carbs – 6.

A lot of people do not like onions, but it adds so much flavor. Chopped fine they "disappear".

Poblano Chicken

6 – 8 cup servings

1 whole chicken
1 poblano pepper – seeded and chopped fine
3 jalapeno peppers – seeded and chopped fine
**Always use latex or nitrile gloves when handling
peppers or they will make your hands feel like
they are on fire.**
1 medium onion – chopped fine
3 medium cloves garlic – chopped fine
16 ounce can Bush's Black Bean Fiesta
2 – 3 tablespoon olive oil

Bake chicken at 350° in covered dish for 2 hours.
Remove from pan and let cool until easily handled.
Sauté peppers, onions, and garlic in olive oil for
about 10 – 15 minutes over medium heat. Remove
chicken from bone and shred. Add to peppers. Add
Black Bean Fiesta and heat thoroughly.

Calories – 166. Fat – 8. Protein – 21. Carbs – 0.
Add beans:
Calories – 18. Fat – 1. Protein – 5. Carbs – 21.
Total:
Calories – 184. Fat – 9. Protein – 26. Carbs – 21.

Shredded or Pulled Chicken

6 – 8 servings – 4 ounces cooked chicken

1 whole chicken
1 tablespoon seasoning salt
½ tablespoon garlic powder
½ tablespoon onion powder
½ tablespoon pepper
½ tablespoon smoke paprika

Place chicken in covered baking dish. Mix spices together and sprinkle over chicken. Bake at 350° for 2 hours. Remove from pan and let cool on platter.

Calories – 166. Fat – 8. Protein – 21. Carbs – 0.

Roast Chicken or Turkey

4 ounces – serving varies by size of bird

1 whole chicken
or
1 whole turkey
2 stalk celery per pound bird
1 small onion per pound bird
seasoning salt to taste
pepper to taste
baking bad

Stuff celery and onion in cavity of cleaned bird, sprinkle with salt and pepper, place in baking bag following directions on box and bake per time according to weight of bird.

Calories – 166. Fat – 8. Protein – 21. Carbs – 0.

Steakhouse Chicken

8 servings – 4 ounces

4 boneless skinless chicken breast
Cut in half lengthwise
just under ½ cup Hellman's Olive Oil mayo
just under ¼ cup ranch dressing
2 tablespoons A1 sauce
8 slices bacon – cooked and crumbled
1 cup shredded cheddar cheese
Optional
4 green onions – thinly sliced

Mix mayo, ranch dressing, and A1. Place in bag with chicken to coat evenly. Grill on medium/hot grill for about 3 – 4 minutes per side. Place on platter and immediately top with bacon crumbles and cheese.

Calories – 304. Fat – 18. Protein – 30. Carbs - <1.

Grilled Pork

3 ounce pork loin or chop

Sprinkle with just plain salt and pepper to taste and grill over medium heat about 5 minutes per side.

I generally treat pork loin like steak, adding steak sauce, rubs, seasoning salt, Liquid Smoke, or whatever the preference. Buying it in a large piece is usually cheaper and meat departments will slice it for you but, I prefer to do it myself.

Calories – 172. Fat – 7. Protein – 26. Carbs – 0.

Grilled Pork w/Roasted Habanero Pineapple Sauce

6 – 3 ounce pork loin

1 packet mushroom gravy
¾ cup water
¼ cup roasted habanero pineapple salsa

On medium heat, grill pork loin for about 5 minutes each side. While pork is resting, prepare mushroom gravy in a saucepan as directed on packet. Add salsa and heat through. Cut pork into ½" – 1" pieces and add to sauce. Combine and heat pork.

Calories – 205. Fat – 7. Protein – 26. Carbs – 8.

Mongolian Pork

6 – 1 cup servings

6 – 3 ounce pork loin cut into ¼" X 2" strips
2 cups coarsely chopped broccoli
½ cup finely chopped onion
2 tablespoons olive oil
2 eggs
¼ cup Mongolian Sauce

In wok, cook pork in oil on medium heat, stirring often for about 10 minutes. Remove from pan and cook broccoli and onion for about 5 – 6 minutes in juices in pan, adding a little more oil if needed. Return pork to pan. Add eggs and let sit for a minute until egg starts to set up. Stir eggs and cook through. When eggs are cooked, stir in Mongolian Sauce.

Mongolian Sauce

6 – ¼ cup servings

1 teaspoon olive oil
½ teaspoon ginger powder
1 tablespoon minced garlic
½ cup soy sauce

½ cup water
1/8 cup brown sugar
½ teaspoon corn starch
cayenne pepper to taste

Warm oil in saucepan over medium/low heat. Add ginger and garlic, stirring quickly to avoid scorching. Add water, soy, corn starch, and brown sugar, allowing sugar to dissolve. Simmer until desired consistency is achieved. Add cayenne pepper to taste.

Calories – 212. Fat – 7. Protein – 27. Carbs – 13.

A lot of people do not like onion but they add so much flavor. Chopped fine they "disappear".

Pulled Pork

About 12 – ½ cup servings

3 pounds pork shoulder or butt
pork rub
2 tablespoon Liquid Smoke
baking bag

Rub favorite rub all over roast and place in baking bag. Bake at 350° for 3 ½ - 4 hours. Remove from bag and let cool until easy to handle. Shred while warm.

Calories – 281. Fat – 12. Protein – 36. Carbs – 0.

Roast Pork

6 – 3 ounce servings

1 ½ pounds pork loin, butt end
seasoning salt and pepper to taste

Place roast in covered baking dish. Sprinkle with salt and pepper. Bake at 350° for 1 ½ - 2 hours. Let rest for 5 minutes before slicing.

Calories – 217. Fat – 13. Protein – 23. Carbs – 0.

Fish

General counts are about the same for any species of fish, whether steamed, grilled, or baked. Calories and fat in salmon, sardines, tuna, or any fish rich in Omega 3 fats are higher but still zero carbs.

3 ounce serving of cod:

Calories – 89. Fat – 1. Protein – 20. Carbs – 0.

Fish Tacos

3 ounces per 1 tortilla:
Calories – 345. Fat – 18 ½. Protein – 29. Carbs – 8.

With 2 fish sticks:
Calories – 340. Fat – 21 ½. Protein – 11. Carbs – 16.

1 low carb tortilla (Santa Fe brand or Tumaros brand)
3 ounces cod – I prefer to grill, but you can substitute
fish sticks to make it super quick, and kids love the
fish sticks.

1 tablespoon Fish Taco Sauce
1 ounce shredded Mexican cheese
1 tablespoon salsa
shredded lettuce
½ tablespoon butter
½ teaspoon garlic salt (melt butter and stir in garlic
salt or garlic powder if avoiding sodium)

Soak bamboo skewers in water. Insert 2 skewers into
3 ounce cod filet, brush with garlic butter. Grill over
medium heat for 3 – 4 minutes each side.

Warm tortilla in microwave for 15 – 20 seconds. Coat
with Fish Taco Sauce.

Layer cod, lettuce, salsa, and cheese.

Fish Taco Sauce

½ tablespoon per small soft taco

3 tablespoon Hellman's Olive Oil mayo
1 teaspoon cayenne pepper
¼ teaspoon chili powder
1/8 teaspoon cumin
dash lemon juice

Mix well.

Calories – 30. Fat – 3. Protein – 0. Carbs – 0.

Tuna

If you have fresh tuna, oh boy! But, everyone knows tuna comes in a can. Never buy tuna in oil if they even still do that. Most popular things to do with tuna are tuna salad sandwiches or tuna casserole. Yes, diabetics can have tuna sandwiches and tuna casserole, using low carb bread or pasta.

Tuna, drained right out of the can – 2 servings
Calories – 50. Fat – 1. Protein – 10. Carbs - <1.

Add to salad, buttered veggies, low carb pasta, and sauce, and calculate nutritional values.

Basic Tuna Salad

2 servings

1 can tuna
2 tablespoon Hellman's Olive Oil mayo

Calories – 80. Fat – 4. Protein – 10. Carbs - <1.

Put on low carb toast or put on salad veggies, or low carb pasta and calculate values. Stuffed in a fresh tomato is good!

Shrimp

Plain cooked shrimp – 4 ounces per serving

Calories – 80. Fat – 0. Protein – 18. Carbs – 0.

I love shrimp and it can be eaten cold as a shrimp cocktail (tasty snack) or in a salad. Shrimp can be used in sauces over Dreamfields pasta, mixed with butter and vegetables in a low carb tortilla. The possibilities are numerous. Even though they have no carbs, be careful to count the carbs of whatever you are adding to them, and the portion of what you are adding them to.

Following are just a few of my favorites.

Grilled Shrimp Kabobs

1 serving

4 ounces shrimp – peeled and deveined
¼ cup zucchini – cut into ¼" slices
¼ cup mushrooms – ¼" slices
Garlic butter sauce

Arrange shrimp and veggies on skewer. Brush with garlic butter sauce.

Grill over medium heat 2 minutes each side or until shrimp is pink.

Calories – 91. Fat – 0. Protein – 18. Carbs – 2.

Shrimp Scampi

4 – 4 ounces per serving

1 pound peeled and deveined shrimp
3 cloves minced garlic
2 tablespoons butter
1 tablespoon olive oil
2 tablespoons flour
1 tablespoon parsley flakes

Lightly dust shrimp in flour, shake off all excess. Melt butter on medium heat in skillet with olive oil. Add garlic and parsley and stir for 1 minute. Add shrimp and cook until pink, stirring every minute.

Calories – 160. Fat – 10. Protein – 18. Carbs – 0.

Scallops

Steamed, baked, grilled – 3 ounces

Calories – 95. Fat – 1. Protein – 20. Carbs – 3.

Living on seafood would be fine by me, but price keeps me from it.

Scallops can also be used in pretty much the same dishes as shrimp except not cold. Someone else may like them in salad but I'm not a fan.

All Other Shellfish

King crab, snow crab, blue crab, oysters, clams, and others I may have missed, generally have zero carbs, no more than a couple as long as they are steamed, grilled, or baked. A cup of oysters has about 10 carbs. It's the highest carb count I've found of any kind of seafood. Not including breaded of course.

Always count carbs of whatever you are eating them with.

Tuna Casserole

6 servings

2 cans tuna – drained
4 - ¾" bundles Dreamfields pasta – cook as directed
on package
4 ounces Baby Bella mushrooms – sliced
4 tablespoons butter
2 tablespoons parmesan cheese
4 ounces lite sour cream

Melt butter over medium/low heat in a large enough pan to eventually add all ingredients. Sauté mushrooms. Stir in parmesan cheese and sour cream, stirring until well blended. Add pasta and tuna, mix well and transfer to baking dish. Bake at 350° for 30 – 45 minutes.

Calories – 270. Fat – 11 ½. Protein – 14. Carbs – 6.

Salads

Walmart has a 4 piece set of pans to make tortilla bowls for 10 bucks. I put the 6 carb multigrain tortillas in and bake them. Great for Taco salad, or any other salad for that matter.

Choose your greens and add your choice of meat, cheese, eggs, veggies, or pretty much anything you like, just count the portions and nutritional values.

Here are some of my favorites:

Taco Salad

1 taco bowl shell (see previous section)
4 ounces warmed taco meat
Lettuce
4 black olives – sliced
1 ounce shredded cheese
3 tablespoons salsa
3 tablespoons lite sour cream

Layer in bowl: lettuce – meat – olives – salsa – sour cream – cheese. Break off bits of bowl to eat with each bite.

With Santa Fe tortilla:
Calories – 538. Fat – 34. Protein – 37. Carbs – 16.

With Tumaros tortilla:
Calories – 498. Fat – 32 ½. Protein – 34. Carbs – 16.

Artichoke Tomato Mozzarella Salad

½ cup artichoke hearts – broken into pieces
6 cherry tomatoes – halved
1 ounce mozzarella chunks
2 tablespoons lite Italian dressing

Mix all together.

Calories – 184. Fat – 9 ½. Protein – 8. Carbs – 17.

Add some low carb pasta if you like, but remember to add nutritional values!

Chapter 6 – Miscellaneous

Hot dogs – Kahns – 1 hot dog no bun
Calories – 150. Fat – 13. Protein – 6. Carbs – 2.

Bratwurst – Johnsonville – 1 wiener no bun
Calories – 260. Fat – 21. Protein – 14. Carbs – 2.

All other various meats that are not generally eaten on a regular basis unless it is in a certain culture. Veal, lamb, and liver are a few. If these are something you like, remember to count portions and nutritional values in entire dish.

3 ounces braised veal cutlet
Calories – 179. Fat – 5. Protein – 31. Carbs – 0.

3 ounces braised lean lamb chop
Calories – 237. Fat – 12. Protein – 30. Carbs – 0.

3 ounces fried liver
Calories – 184. Fat – 7. Protein – 23. Carbs – 7.

Chapter 7 – Breads and Sides

Sandwich Thins (multigrain)
Calories – 100. Fat – 1. Protein – 4. Carbs – 18.

Regular sandwich bun
Calories – 140. Fat – 1 ½. Protein – 4. Carbs – 25.

Low carb wheat bread – 2 slices
Calories – 70. Fat – ½. Protein – 5. Carbs – 16.

Regular wheat bread – 2 slices
Calories – 240. Fat – 3. Protein – 10. Carbs – 46.

Tortilla – 1
Small:
Calories – 90. Fat – 2. Protein – 2. Carbs – 16.
Medium ;
Calories – 140. Fat – 3 ½. Protein – 4. Carbs – 24.
Large:
Calories – 200. Fat – 4 ½. Protein – 5. Carbs – 34.

Low carb (varies by brand) – Santa Fe Company
Calories – 100. Fat – 3 ½. Protein – 8. Carbs – 6.

Low carb (varies by brand) – Tumaros
Calories – 60. Fat – 2. Protein – 5. Carbs – 6.

Crescent
Calories – 200. Fat – 12. Protein – 2. Carbs – 22.

4" plain bagel
Calories – 245. Fat – 1. Protein – 9. Carbs – 46.

Biscuit – Buttery Flakey Big Grands
Calories – 170. Fat – 6. Protein – 3. Carbs – 25

4" pita
Calories – 77. Fat – trace. Protein – 3. Carbs – 16.

Bagel thin
Calories – 110. Fat – 1. Protein – 5. Carbs – 24.

Dreamfield's pasta (check with nutritionist if they approve and recommend this)
Calories – 190. Fat – 1. Protein – 7. Carbs – 5 digestible carbs.

Potatoes – baked without skin (21/3" X 4 ¾")
Calories – 145. Fat – trace. Protein – 3. Carbs – 34.

Twice baked potato – 2 servings per potato

Bake washed potato (pierce skin with fork in several places so it doesn't explode) at 350° for 45 minutes to 1 hour. Cut in half lengthwise, scoop out flesh and place in bowl. Mash with 1 tablespoon butter, 1 tablespoon lite sour cream, and 1 ounce cheddar cheese (or your favorite cheese) per potato. Return mixture to skins and bake at 350° for 30 minutes.

Calories – 202. Fat – 11. Protein – 6. Carbs – 18.

Remember, this is half of a whole potato.

French fries – 9 to 10 fries
Calories – 80. Fat – 3 ½. Protein – 1. Carbs – 12.

Tater rounds – 11 pieces
Calories – 160. Fat – 8. Protein – 2. Carbs – 21.

Veggies

Kids are generally not fond of veggies, so good luck with this. They do have carbs so make sure to check the carb count if it is a veggie they like.

Cole slaw and salads – nutrition count depends on type.

Soups – nutrition counts depends on type, some have very low carbs.

White rice – ¾ cup prepared
Calories – 154. Fat – 0. Protein – 3. Carbs – 34.

Penne pasta – 2 ounces dry
Calories – 200. Fat – 1. Protein – 7. Carbs – 42.

Sauces

Adobe Sauce

If you like spicy, just take a small can of chipotle peppers in adobe sauce and chop it up fine. Add to just about anything you want to add some flavorful zing to. This is with mayo.

½ teaspoon chopped chipotle
1 tablespoon Hellman's Olive Oil mayo

Calories – 62. Fat – 6. Protein – 0. Carbs – 1.

Alfredo Sauce

8 servings

1 stick of butter
1 tablespoon minced garlic
¼ cup parmesan cheese
2 eggs – beaten
8 ounces lite sour cream
4 ounces milk
2 tablespoons parsley

Melt butter in saucepan over medium/low heat. Sauté garlic for 2 – 3 minutes. Stir in parmesan cheese. Stir in remaining ingredients and heat until it just starts to boil.

Calories – 193. Fat – 17. Protein – 4. Carbs – 4.

Add 16 ounces of crab, fresh or imitation, and serve over linguini noodles, regular or low carb depending on how many carbs are needed for that time of day.

Avocado Lime Sauce

8 – 2 tablespoon servings

1 ripe avocado
1 tablespoon Hellman's Olive Oil mayo
1 tablespoon lime juice
salt and pepper to taste

Peel and pit avocado. Mash and stir together with mayo and lime juice. Refrigerate.

Good on burgers, grilled chicken, salads, fish . . . but I love avocado.

Calories – 39. Fat – 3 ½. Protein - <1. Carbs – 1.

Basic Red Meat Sauce

9 – ½ cup servings

2 pounds ground beef – extra lean
1 pound pork sausage
2 – 15 ounce cans diced tomatoes
2 – 15 ounce cans tomato sauce
2 large cloves minced garlic
1 medium – chopped
¼ cup red wine
2 teaspoons basil
2 teaspoons oregano
2 tablespoons parsley
2 tablespoons sugar
salt and pepper to taste

On medium heat, brown meats in large pan. Drain all fat. Add garlic and onion and cook for about 10 minutes, stirring every 2 minutes. Add tomatoes and wine, allow to cook down (about 15 minutes). Add remaining ingredients and bring to a boil. Reduce heat to low, cover, and simmer for 2 hours.

Calories – 206. Fat – 13. Protein – 16. Carbs – 7.

Cajun Rub

This makes enough for 1 rub and has little to no nutritional value except small traces, mostly sodium.

2 teaspoons salt
2 teaspoons garlic powder
2 ½ teaspoons smoked paprika
1 teaspoon black pepper
1 teaspoon cayenne pepper
1 ¼ teaspoon oregano
½ teaspoon thyme
1 teaspoon red pepper flakes

Mix all together and rub into all sides of chosen meat, place in bag and let marinate overnight.

Cocktail Sauce

8 – ½ teaspoon servings

4 tablespoons ketchup
3 teaspoons horseradish
½ teaspoons lemon juice

Mix well.

Calories – 12. Fat - <1. Protein – 0. Carbs – 3.

Cole Slaw Dressing

8 servings

> 4 tablespoon Hellman's Olive Oil mayo
> ½ cup Lite Sweet Vidalia Onion salad dressing

Mix well.

Calories – 70. Fat – 5. Protein – 0. Carbs – 6.

Enchilada Sauce

8 – ½ cup servings

1 tablespoon olive oil
3 cloves garlic – minced
¼ small onion – minced
½ teaspoon oregano
2 ½ teaspoons chili powder
1 ½ teaspoons cayenne pepper
¼ teaspoons salt
¼ teaspoon cumin
1 tablespoon parsley
1 ½ teaspoon Liquid Smoke
16 ounces tomato sauce
1 ½ cups chicken broth
2 tablespoon flour
1/8 cup tequila

Heat oil in large saucepan over medium heat. Add garlic and onion and sauté for 1 – 2 minutes. Add spices and tomato sauce. Mix well. Add flour to chicken broth and stir constantly until it comes to a boil. Stir in tequila and simmer for 20 minutes.

Calories – 36. Fat – 0. Protein – 0. Carbs – 5.

Fish Taco Sauce

6 servings – ½ tablespoon per small soft taco

3 tablespoons Hellman's Olive Oil mayo
1 teaspoon cayenne pepper
¼ teaspoon chili powder
1/8 teaspoon cumin
dash lemon juice

Mix well.

Calories – 30. Fat – 3. Protein – 0. Carbs – 0.

Garlic Butter Sauce

8 servings

½ cup butter
1 teaspoon Worcestershire sauce
1 tablespoon lemon juice
1 clove garlic – crushed
1 tablespoon parmesan cheese
½ tablespoon dry white wine

Melt butter in saucepan, sauté garlic for 1 minute. Add remaining ingredients and cook for 1 minute.

Calories – 104. Fat – 11. Protein <1. Carbs – 0.

Guacamole

8 – 12 servings

3 ripe avocados – peeled and pitted
1 lime – juice of
1 teaspoon salt
¼ cup finely chopped onion
2 diced plum tomatoes
1 teaspoon minced garlic
¼ teaspoon pepper – cayenne if you want a little kick

Mix well.

Calories – 100. Fat – 9. Protein – 0. Carbs – 3.

Honey Mustard Sauce

8 – 1 tablespoon servings

¼ cup Hellman's Olive Oil mayo
2 tablespoon yellow mustard
2 tablespoon honey

Mix well.

Calories – 45. Fat – 3. Protein – 0. Carbs – 2.

Marinara Sauce

8 – ½ cup servings

16 ounce can tomato sauce
16 ounce can crushed or diced tomatoes
2 tablespoons sugar
2 teaspoons oregano
1 teaspoon garlic salt
1 teaspoon basil
2 teaspoons parsley
2 teaspoons red pepper flakes

Combine all ingredients in a saucepan, bring to boil and simmer for 45 minutes – 1 hour.

Calories – 38. Fat – 0. Protein <1. Carbs – 8.

Mongolian Sauce

6 – ¼ cup servings

1 teaspoon olive oil
½ teaspoon ginger powder
1 tablespoon minced garlic
½ cup soy sauce
½ cup water
1/8 cup brown sugar
½ teaspoon corn starch
cayenne pepper

Warm oil in saucepan over medium/low heat. Add ginger and sugar. Stir quickly to avoid scorching. Add water, soy, and sugar, allowing sugar to dissolve. Simmer until desired consistency is reached. Add cayenne pepper to taste.

Calories – 103. Fat – 0. Protein <1. Carbs – 26.

Queso Chorizo Dip

8 – 3 ½ cup servings

4 ounces chorizo sausage
8 ounces shredded Mexi-blend cheese
8 ounces cream cheese
¾ cup milk
1 cup medium to hot salsa – to taste

Cook chorizo over medium/high heat, stirring and browning well and breaking up lumps (about 5 minutes). Drain on paper towels. Melt cheeses and milk together in double boiler, microwave, or saucepan (careful not to scorch). Any method requires frequent stirring. Place in crockpot or fondue to keep warm.

Calories – 260. Fat – 22. Protein – 11. Carbs – 5.

Refried Bean Sauce

6 servings

1 can refried beans
1 ¾ cup chicken broth
1 tablespoon chili powder
1 tablespoon red pepper flakes
¼ cup queso or Mexi-blend shredded cheese

Heat in saucepan, stirring regularly until well blended. Serve over pork, beef, or chicken with salsa and sour cream.

Calories – 134. Fat – 4. Protein – 12. Carbs – 10.

Salsa Sauce

Individual serving

2 tablespoon salsa
1 tablespoon sour cream

Mix together and use as a topping or dressing.

Calories – 33. Fat – 2. Protein – 0. Carbs – 3.

Spinach Artichoke Dip

12 servings

16 ounces spinach – cooked and drained
1 tablespoon olive oil
2 tablespoons minced garlic
2 cups artichokes – squeezed and drained
2 cups Hellman's Olive Oil mayo
2 cups Swiss cheese
¼ cup parmesan cheese – topping

Sauté garlic in olive oil. Mix in remaining ingredients and top with parmesan cheese. Bake in 9" pie pan at 350° for 30 minutes.

Calories – 240. Fat – 21. Protein – 1 ½. Carbs – 3 ½.

Taco Seasoning

6 servings – 3 tablespoons per 1 cup of water

9 tablespoons corn starch
3 tablespoons chili powder
1 ½ teaspoons salt
1 ½ teaspoon pepper
¾ teaspoons garlic powder
¾ teaspoons onion powder
¾ teaspoons oregano
1 ½ teaspoon smoke paprika
1 ½ teaspoons cumin
1 ½ teaspoons cayenne pepper

Mix all together and store in an airtight container.

Calories – 54. Fat – 0. Protein – 0. Carbs – 13.

Tartar Sauce

1 tablespoon servings

1 tablespoon Hellman's Olive Oil mayo
1 teaspoon sweet relish

Mix well.

Calories – 66. Fat – 6. Protein – 0. Carbs – 2.

Veggie Sauce

8 servings

1 cup cooked mashed veggies (cauliflower, broccoli,
carrots, or a mix of veggies)
4 tablespoons butter
2 tablespoon parmesan cheese
4 ounces sour cream

Melt butter and stir in parmesan. Add sour cream and
cook to a bubble. Add veggies and heat through.

These values are using cauliflower – other veggies
vary slightly.

Calories – 93. Fat – 8. Protein – 1 ½. Carbs – 1 ½.

Snacks

Justin and his mom bag up dry snacks in snack bags, all of one type or mixing different things to equal about 15 carbs per bag. They do the same for refrigerated items. These are some of the snacks he likes:

Popcorn – 1 cup
Calories – 25. Fat – 7. Protein – 2. Carbs – 16.

Lance peanut butter and cheese crackers – 1 square
Calories – 34. Fat – 2. Protein <1. Carbs – 2 ½.

Cheez-Its – 27 crackers
Calories – 150. Fat – 8. Protein – 3. Carbs – 16

½ peanut butter sandwich – 1 tablespoon peanut butter and low carb bread
Calories – 130. Fat – 8. Protein – 9. Carbs – 7.

Quaker cheddar rice snacks – 18 mini cakes
Calories – 140. Fat – 5. Protein – 2. Carbs – 20.

Sunflower seed – ¼ cup
Calories – 200. Fat – 17. Protein – 7. Carbs – 4.

1 mini chocolate bar
Calories – 42. Fat – 2 ½. Protein - <1. Carbs – 5.

Pretzels – 20 small sticks
Calories – 22. Fat – trace. Protein – trace. Carbs – 4.

Goldfish – 57 fish
Calories – 140. Fat – 5. Protein – 4. Carbs – 17.

Pringles – 16 crisps
Calories – 150. Fat – 9. Protein – 1. Carbs – 14.

Tostitos – 13 chips
Calories – 140. Fat – 7. Protein – 2. Carbs – 18.

Nuts – 1 ounce peanuts (about 28 nuts)
Calories – 166. Fat – 14. Protein – 7. Carbs – 4.

Pork rinds – ½ ounce
Calories – 76. Fat – 4. Protein – 9. Carbs – 0.

Cinnamon mini Streusel Muffin – 1 mini muffin
Calories – 52 ½. Fat – 2. Protein - <1. Carbs – 8.

Refrigerated Snacks

Sugar-free fat-free puddings. Prepare as directed on package. Pour into ½ cup Gladware (perfect for saving and serving).

Calories – 80. Fat – 0. Protein - <1. Carbs – 8.

Deviled eggs – 1 egg (half of a whole). Boil however many eggs you want to prepare in a pan for about 10 minutes. Cool completely, peel, and slice in half lengthwise. Scoop out yolk and smash in ½ tablespoon Hellman's Olive Oil mayo and ½ teaspoon yellow mustard. Salt and pepper to taste. Spoon or use cake decorator to return mixture to egg white. Chill

Calories – 50 Fat – 3. Protein – 3. Carbs – 0.

Celery and peanut butter – 1 stalk and 2 tablespoons
Calories – 196. Fat – 16. Protein – 7. Carbs – 9.

Apple slices and peanut butter – 1 apple and 2 tablespoons
Calories – 285.Fat – 16. Protein – 7 ½. Carbs – 28 ½.

Fruits – again, Gladware is perfect to store ½ cup

servings

Pineapple
Calories – 60. Fat – 0. Protein – 0. Carbs – 15

Peaches
Calories – 70. Fat – 0. Protein – 1. Carbs – 17.

Pears
Calories – 62. Fat – 0. Protein – ½. Carbs – 16.

Fruit cocktail
Calories – 155. Fat – 0. Protein – ½. Carbs – 14 ½.

Apple – 1 medium fresh (3" diameter)
Calories – 95. Fat – ½. Protein – ½. Carbs – 20 ½.

Orange – 1 medium fresh (2 ½" diameter)
Calories – 62. Fat – ½. Protein – 1 ½. Carbs – 15 ½.

Pears – 1 medium fresh (2 ½" diameter)
Calories – 96. Fat – ½. Protein – ½. Carbs – 20 ½.

Banana – 1 medium (7" – 7 ½" long)
Calories – 105. Fat – ½. Protein – 1 ½. Carbs – 24.

Grapes – 10 to 12 grapes
Calories – 36. Fat – 0. Protein – 0. Carbs – 8 ½.

Fruit smoothies 2 – 12 ounce servings.
6 ounces plain yogurt

1 cup frozen fruit
8 ounces V8 Fusion
Blend on high until milkshake consistency.
Calories – 140. Fat – 0. Protein – 9. Carbs – 24.

Yogurt – 6 ounces plain fat-free
Calories – 100. Fat – 0. Protein – 18. Carbs – 7.

Cottage Cheese – ½ cup
Calories – 110. Fat – 4 ½. Protein – 12. Carbs – 5.

1 baby carrot
Calories – 4. Fat – 0. Protein – 0. Carbs – 1.

1 cup cauliflower
Calories – 25. Fat – 0. Protein – 0. Carbs – 5.

1 celery stalk
Calories – 6. Fat – 0. Protein – 0. Carbs – 1.

Shrimp cocktail – ½ teaspoon per shrimp w/12 cooked shrimp (peeled and deveined)
Calories – 92. Fat – 0. Protein – 18. Carbs – 3.

Tyson buffalo chicken tenders – 3 ounces
Calories – 180. Fat – 8. Protein – 15. Carbs – 14.

Pig in a blanket – wrap 1 cocktail wiener in half a crescent. Bake as directed on package.
Calories – 78. Fat – 5. Protein – 1. Carbs – 6.

Graham cracker "ice cream" sandwich – 1 whole graham cracker broken into 4 sections. 2 tablespoons Cool Whip. Spread Cool Whip between crackers and freeze. Store frozen "sandwich" in sealed freezer bag.

Calories – 89. Fat – 4 ½. Protein – 1 ½. Carbs – 8.

Individual brownie – 1 serving
1 tablespoon flour
1 tablespoon sugar
1 tablespoon cocoa powder
Pinch baking soda
Pinch salt
2 tablespoons plain fat-free yogurt you may need to add a bit more to make it blend well)
½ teaspoon vanilla
Mix all together and place on parchment paper in microwave. Cook on high power for about 1 minute.
Calories – 116. Fat – 1. Protein – 7. Carbs – 23.

Sample Menus

The following sample menus are based on the nutritional values for my grandson, an active 13 year old teenager. Each person's needs will vary.

6:30am – Breakfast – 30 to 45 carbs

12:00 noon – Lunch – 75 to 90 carbs

3:30pm – Afternoon Snack – 15 carbs

5:30pm – Dinner – 30 to 45 carbs

8:00pm – Evening Snack – 15 carbs

Week One

Remember, you are cooking as much of this as you can on Sunday so it's easy to grab or heat up and go.

Breakfast

Frittata – 0 carbs
Smoothie – 24 carbs
2 slices low carb buttered toast – 16 carbs
Total – 40 carbs

Lunch Monday/Wednesday

Ham and cheese on bun – 25 carbs
1 cup vegetable soup – 24 carbs
Apple – 21 carbs
Total – 70 carbs

Lunch Tuesday/Thursday

2 hot dogs on buns w/ketchup – 56 carbs
Banana – 24 carbs
Total – 70 carbs

Afternoon Snacks

Choose from bagged snack storage – 15 carbs

Lunch Friday

Tuna salad on regular wheat bread – 46 carbs
Chips from snack storage – 15 carbs
Brownie – 23 carbs
Total – 84 carbs

Dinner Monday/Wednesday

Baked chicken – 0 carbs
Baked potato w/butter and sour cream – 34 carbs
Total – 34 carbs

Dinner Tuesday/Thursday

Vegetable soup – 24 carbs
Grilled cheese on low carb bread – 16 carbs
Total – 40 carbs

Dinner Friday

Cheeseburger – 25 carbs
15 fries – 20 carbs
Total – 45 carbs

Evening Snacks

3 pigs in a blanket each night – 18 carbs

Week Two

Breakfast

Ham, egg, and cheese on sandwich thin – 18 carbs
Smoothie – 24 carbs
Total – 42 carbs

Lunch Monday/Wednesday

2 buns with choice of lunch meat – 50 carbs
1 cup peaches – 30 carbs
Total – 80 carbs

Lunch Tuesday/Thursday

2 medium burritos w/beans, sauce, taco meat, and cheese – 74 carbs
Total – 74 carbs

Lunch Friday

Meatballs w/ regular penne pasta in Basic Red Meat Sauce w/crescent roll – 82 carbs
Total – 82 carbs

Afternoon Snacks

Choose from bagged snack storage – 15 carbs

Dinner Monday/Wednesday

Basic Red Meat Sauce and meatballs over low carb pasta – 20 carbs
Toasted hamburger buns w/garlic butter – 25 carbs
Total – 45 carbs

Dinner Tuesday/Thursday

Mongolian chicken w/3/4 cup rice – 40 carbs
Total – 40 carbs

Dinner Friday

Fish tacos – 2 small tortillas made with 2 fish sticks each – 32 carbs
Total – 32 carbs

Evening Snacks

Beef jerky – 0 carbs

About the Author

Arianna has been cooking for her family and friends for most of her life. When she was diagnosed with breast cancer, her family and friends got to cook for her. With that loving support and a positive outlook, she won her battle against cancer, and regained her health.

She can now be found dancing around her house with her husband, listening to Dean Martin, and drinking wine. And cooking, of course.

She is also the author of:

**Cooking Ahead: The less Stress Way
To Cook For 2 To 200**

To contact the author: ariannaguinn@gmail.com

If you liked this book, please review it and take the time to tell your friends and family.

Thank you.

14011502R00065

Printed in Poland
by Amazon Fulfillment
Poland Sp. z o.o., Wrocław